The Craftsman's Art Series

The Craft of
Soft Furnishing

Anne Van Wyke

Stanley Paul, London

Stanley Paul & Co Ltd
3 Fitzroy Square, London W1P 6JD

An imprint of the Hutchinson Publishing Group

London Melbourne Sydney Auckland
Wellington Johannesburg and agencies
throughout the world

First published 1978
© Anne Van Wyke 1978
Drawings © Stanley Paul & Co Ltd 1978

Set in Monotype Times

Printed in Great Britain by litho at
The Anchor Press Ltd, and bound by
Wm Brendon & Son Ltd, both of
Tiptree, Essex

ISBN 0 09 131670 7 (cased)
      0 09 131671 5 (paper)

Contents

Introduction

Clever soft furnishing can transform any home, but today's high labour costs are making it essential for more and more people to learn some of the skills involved. This book gives step by step help to success on all the basics and some more advanced techniques too. There are clear instructions on making piping, cushions, lampshades and curtains. There is a clear and detailed chapter on that most daunting task, making a loose cover.

Soft furnishing is an enjoyable hobby, not to be confused with upholstery, where you are stripping the fabric down to the wood, using special tools and under an expert's guidance. All you require is a sewing machine, some skill in its use, good materials and a willing pair of hands.

1.Cushions

Making your own cushions is one of the most simple ways to start learning the art of soft furnishing. Several types are possible: hard shaped cushions for armchairs, and scatter cushions or circular cushions.

Hard cushion with boxed corners

REQUIREMENTS

Dunlopillo or foam rubber, 7.5–10cm/3–4in. thickness, cut to the exact size.
Calico or a lining material to cover the rubber to prevent it deteriorating and rubbing apart. For a cushion 61 × 58cm/24 × 23in., 10cm/4in. thick you will require about 140cm/55in. of fabric.
Thread, preferably cotton as you are using a cotton fabric.
Scissors, pins, a needle. If you are having to cut the rubber to size yourself (some shops will cut to your specific measurements) you will need a serrated knife, like a bread knife.
Paper, to make a pattern the shape of the seat.

Make a paper pattern by placing it on the seat, and use a pencil to draw around the shape. Cut it out, and place it back on, to check that it is exact.

Lay the pattern onto the foam rubber, and draw around it with a ballpoint or felt pen. Cut the foam with the serrated-edge knife, using it with the same movement you would use to cut a loaf of bread. Make sure as you are cutting that the knife is at right-angles with the top of the cushion. This avoids a sloping edge. If you have to use a large pair of scissors, use the longest cuts possible, as you will find that scissors leave a ridged edge which can be visible if you are covering it with a fine material.

The cover can be made in two ways.

1. Cut the material in a rectangular shape, first measuring from the back, across the top and down around to the back again, adding

2.5cm/1in. for seams. Next measure the width plus half of the depth either side, adding again 2.5cm/1in. for seams.

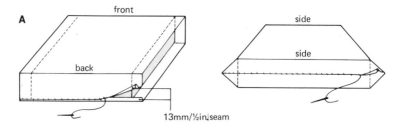

Wrap the lining around cushion, turn under seam allowance at the back base seamline. Oversew by hand with a small hemstitch. Join the sides in the same stitch, with the seam across the centre.

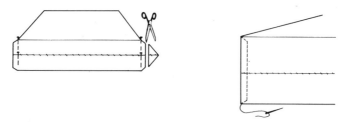

Flatten the corners, pin down the edge, and cut off the extra allowing 13mm/½in. to tuck in; oversew.

2. This second way of covering a 'hard cushion' is more exact, as it enables your seamlines to match those on the cushion. Thus avoiding seams showing through your finished outer cover, if using a fine material.

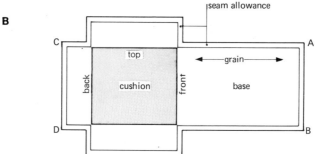

Cutting layout

If you prefer to make a paper pattern first, lay your cushion onto the paper, and wrap the paper around so that the ends meet at the back lower edge. Draw the shape of the top and base edges, fold the paper down the sides, and draw the four corner edges. Remove the cushion, lay the paper out and cut around the shape, allowing 13mm/½in. all round for the seam allowance.

Pin pattern onto lining, and cut around.

Allow 13mm/½in. seam allowance, and turn under all seams as you work them. Start by placing the cushion on the fabric, on the *top* position, fold the base piece over, and join AB to CD first. Use a small hemstitch. Fold the two sides down, turn under seam allowance and stitch along the two sides. Clip the corners, turn under seams and stitch.

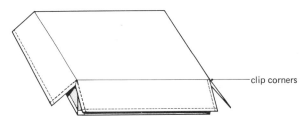
clip corners

Some modern chair cushions have rounded edges, with no piping required for the seams. These can be made from the same type of rubber, but encased in a Terylene wadding, to give that soft rounded effect.

Make a paper pattern of the exact shape of the cushion, but reduce it by 2.5cm/1in. all round. Also purchase a thinner foam rubber than required, as the wadding will add about 2.5cm/1in. to the thickness.

REQUIREMENTS

Foam rubber or Dunlopillo, 2.5cm/1in. thinner than required size. Terylene wadding, enough to wrap completely around the cushion, and overlap down the sides. This can be bought at most large furnishing stores, or failing there, your local upholstery shop will always have some or will advise you.

Pins, and a needle (preferably a size 3 Crewel) or the longest one you have.

Thread, a cotton or synthetic depending on fabric. Use synthetic thread for synthetic fabrics and cotton for natural fabrics.

Wrap the wadding around the foam, starting at the back. Pull it fairly taut, and pin in position, starting at the centre and working outwards. Trim off any excess wadding so that it joins evenly, oversew with large stitches through the wadding, use a herring bone stitch.

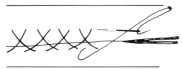

Pin the sides similarly, trimming off the excess wadding both along the sides and the corners, and oversew using the same type of stitch.

This cushion must be covered with either a fine cotton lining or calico, before putting the outer cover on. This prevents the wadding tearing, and keeps it in position. Use the first method A for making this lining.

Scatter cushion

Making your own cushions has the advantage that you can choose the sizes and shapes to suit the materials you are working with, whether they are left-overs, a piece of needlepoint, tapestry, or a piece of patchwork.

Feathers from an old bolster or pillow are the ideal filling. Do not use untreated chicken feathers as they are unpurified, and will eventually smell unpleasant. Foam rubber chippings can be used, but they do tend to look rather lumpy. Kapok is a good and cheap filling, obtainable from most large stores. Terylene wadding can also be used.

Use a fine cotton ticking for the inside cover if you are using feathers, as this is a feather-proof fabric. Calico or a cotton sateen can be used for any of the other fillings.

There are three stages in making the cushion: the inner cover, the filling, and the outer cover.

REQUIREMENTS FOR INNER COVER AND FILLING

Calico or cotton ticking for inner cover. A cotton thread. Filling. Pins. Crewel sewing needle size 9. Scissors.

Circular cushion

If you wish to make a paper pattern first, draw around a circular object, a large dinner plate maybe, and if this is not large enough, enlarge it by using a ruler to mark the extra width the same distance around your first circle. A pencil attached to a piece of string can also be used like a compass. Always make the cushion 2.5cm/1in. larger than required, to give a fuller appearance, and remember to add your seam allowance.

Place pattern on the lining fabric and cut two similar circles. Place right sides together and machine using a small stitch, to prevent any of the filling coming through the seam, leaving an opening of 15–20cm/6–8in., for filling. Turn right side out, and fill. If you are using feathers, you cannot prevent some feathers flying around. It is best to conduct this operation either in an outhouse, garage, or over a water-filled bath. Have your vacuum cleaner handy and tie your hair up in a scarf.

If you are using the feathers from an old pillow, shake the feathers to the bottom, then carefully cut an opening at the top, the size of the opening you have left in your cover.

Pin the pillow edges to the cover edges, as close together as possible (alternatively tack these edges together).

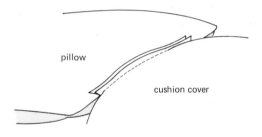

pillow

cushion cover

Gently shake the feathers down into the cover, filling the cushion fuller than required, as they soon squash down, once the air has been plumped out of it.

Remove the pins or tacking, turn the seam inwards and machine the edges together, as near the edge as possible.

When filling with Kapok or foam chippings, make the cover similarly. Fill by hand but do not over fill, close the end with one hand and gently plump the cushion to ensure that it does not become too hard or lumpy looking. Turn edges inside and stitch as before.

Outer covers

These can be elaborated with frills, piping, braid, fringing and buttoning. Buttons, for covering with your own fabric are obtainable in most haberdasheries, or dress material shops, and come in an assortment of sizes; they are sold on cards which give you the instructions on covering them.

Buttoning

When the outer cover is finished, place on the inner cushion and mark the position for the button with a pin. A single button in the centre is most common. Use a button thread (available in the same shops). If they have none, use a double thread of cotton. Pass the needle through your buttoning mark, leaving a length at the back. Pass the needle through the button and tie a knot around it. Pass the needle back again about 6mm/$\frac{1}{4}$in. away from the first thread, through the button, remove the needle and tie the two loose threads together tightly and securely. Cut the ends, not too short, but enough to be hidden behind the button.

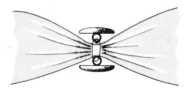

Piping

Piping gives any type of cover a professional finish, as well as making it more hard-wearing by reinforcing the seams. It is simply made from strips of material, cut 4cm/1$\frac{1}{2}$in. wide, on the cross of the fabric to give it elasticity. There are two ways of making it, the first for small amounts, as for cushions, and the second for a large amount ideal for loose covers.

Piping method 1

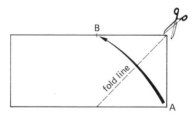

Fold corner A up to meet B at right-angles, make a crease on fold line. Open out, and cut along crease.

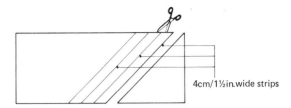

4cm/1½in.wide strips

Cut 4cm/1½in. strips, parallel to your cutting line.

Joining piping strips

right side   right side

Lay two strips, right side up, along side each other.

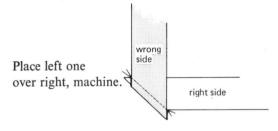

wrong side

right side

Place left one over right, machine.

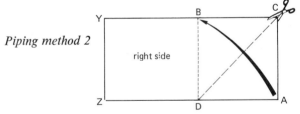

Y   B   C

right side

Z   D   A

Piping method 2

Fold corner A to meet B at right-angles, make a crease on the fold line. Open out and cut along the crease.

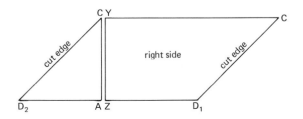

C Y   C

cut edge   right side   cut edge

D₂   A Z   D₁

Place the cut triangular piece of material to the opposite edge, YZ, and machine the two sides together, right sides together. Trim the seam to 6mm/1¼in. open out and press.

Lay the material face down, mark 4cm/1½in. strips with either a pencil or french chalk and ruler.

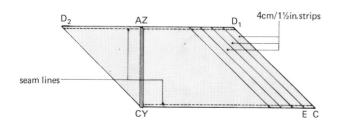

With right sides together pin corner D₁ to point E, which is 4cm/1½in. in, and pin or tack together the seam, forming a tube. Machine seam, and trim to 6mm/¼in.

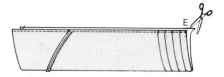

Starting at point E, cut the strips, following your pencil lines. You will find that you have a long, continuous strip of material, with no wastage. This method is the most economical for large items like loose covers.

PIPING CORD

Piping cord is available at most drapers' stores, and is made in sizes ranging from 0 the thinnest, to 6 the thickest. For cushions and loose covers size 4 is normally used, but a lot depends on the thickness of your material, and how bold the effect you require is. When buying the cord, always check that it has been pre-shrunk. If it has not, cut at least one-third more than you require, boil it in a saucepan of water for about three minutes, then hang out to dry. This is important – a beautifully made article can be ruined after the first wash as the shrinkage causes the material to pucker and it cannot be pulled to its original length again.

ASSEMBLING PIPING MATERIAL AND CORD

Place the cord into the centre of the strip of material, wrong side uppermost. Fold the material over the cord, and tack.

It is now ready to be inserted into your prepared article.

JOINING CORD ENDS TOGETHER

1. Untwist about 2.5cm/1in. of either end to be joined.
2.

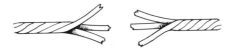

Cut one strand off each end.
3.

Twist the remaining four strands together.
4. Place the twisted cord on to the prepared piping strip and continue as before.

INSERTING PIPING

It is simplest to machine piping first on a cushion cover. This 46cm/18in. square piped cover is easy to make. Whatever shapes you subsequently try, the insertion of piping is always the same.

Piped cushions

REQUIREMENTS

48cm/19in. of 122cm/48in. wide fabric.
Piping cord No. 4 2·06m/2¼yds.
Matching sewing thread, (preferably Drima or a synthetic thread as it has more give, and is stronger, for either a cotton or synthetic fabric).
41cm/16in. zip, or velcro tape.

A completed piped cushion, 46 cm × 46 cm, and material ready for assembly – from half a yard of material you can make the cushion and the lampshade illustrated.

1. Measure and cut two pieces of fabric 48cm/19in. square.

2. Mark the remainder with either a pencil or french chalk, into 4cm/1½in. strips, on the bias, to make a 193cm/76in. strip of piping, when joined together.

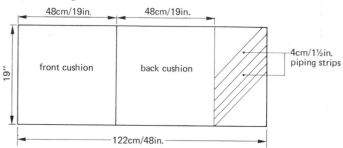

3. Prepare the piping as in *piping method 1*, and insert the cord accordingly.

4. With the right side of fabric uppermost, tack the piping around the edge of one square, on the seam allowance line. Taper the corners slightly so that they are not a sharp right-angle, but more rounded.

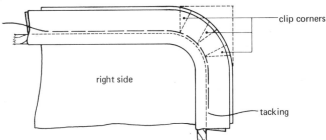

5. Place the other square, face down, onto the right facing side of the prepared square. Tack into position on the seam allowance line, Mark with a pin on either side, the 41cm/16in. gap for the zip or velcro opening.

6. Machine these together, using the 'zipper foot', starting at the zip base, finishing at the zip top.

7. Remove the tacking, trim seams to 6mm/$\frac{1}{4}$in.; clip all curves, and oversew the raw edges.

8. Turn right side out, and pin the seam allowance of the unpiped side under.

9. Open the zip, and pin into position, ensuring the teeth nearest the piped edge are as near the cord as possible.

Using the zipper foot machine the side with the piped edge first, on the seam allowance line.

Machine the other side, with the zip teeth about 6mm/$\frac{1}{4}$in. from the edge.

Oversew the zip edges to the raw edges of the seams.

VELCRO

Velcro is a double tape. One side is made up of a mass of barbs, which adheres securely on contact with the other velvety side. It can be used for a considerable variety of crafts: in dress making in place of zips on skirts; for aprons; or any number of openings. It is available in white, black and beige 15mm/⅝in. wide; an assortment of colours 21mm/⅞in. wide.

It has the advantage of being very simple to apply, or insert, especially in cushions, and it cannot be broken.

VELCRO INSERTION FOR A PIPED CUSHION

After piping the first square, lay both squares right side up, beside each other.

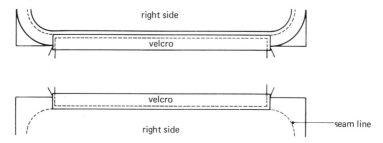

On the piped side, machine the velcro level with the seam allowance line, as close to the piping as possible.

Place the other side also level with the seam line, and machine 3mm/⅛in. outside the line.

Put both sides together, right sides innermost, closing the velcro. Pin and then tack around the cushion sides, omitting the opening.

Machine together, just overlapping either end of the velcro by 6mm/¼in. Remove tacking, trim the seams, and clip all curves. Open velcro, turn right side out, and press.

In place of piping around the cushion, a gathered or pleated frill could look attractive. This is made from 7.5cm/3in. strips of fabric cut on the cross (like the piping strips) joined together to form a strip one and a half times the all-round measurement of the cushion. Double in half lengthwise and loosely gather. Tack around the edge of one side of the cushion and make up, as you would for the piped cushion.

Bolster cushions can look very attractive whether for a Chesterfield settee, or as decoration on the spare bed. These can be covered in most types of firmly-woven fabric. There are two types of bolster cushions, the soft, made from just one length of material and gathered at either end, or a hard, fitted bolster made from a length of material for the main body, with two circular ends, gathered in the centre, and finished off with button or tassel at each end.

INNER COVER AND FILLING FOR BOLSTER CUSHIONS

Any of the fillings used for scatter cushions are suitable for a bolster, except feathers for a hard fitted one. I would suggest Kapok or horse hair (if you have an old horse hair mattress, remove the hair, put it into an old pillow case, knot at the end, and wash thoroughly in warm soapy water. Rinse well, and hang out to dry. Choose a hot sunny day for this, and hang outside away from anything that could become stained). For feathers use a down-proof fabric like a cotton ticking. Use cotton sateen or calico for the other fillings.

Soft bolster

REQUIREMENTS

For a cushion 61cm/24in. long and approx. 23cm/9in. in diameter you will need 91 cm/36in. of 91 cm/36in. wide material.
Approx. 1.6kg/3½lbs of Kapok, or 1.4kg/3lbs. of feathers.
Cotton sewing thread, pins, scissors.

Cut a rectangular piece of material, 63cm/25in. long, 79cm/31in. wide. This is for the main body. Make a paper pattern for the circular ends, 24cm/9½in. in diameter. You will find most small dinner plates are roughly this size. Cut two patterns, one for each end.

With right sides together, fold the rectangle in half, lengthways. Pin together, allowing 13mm/½in. seams, leaving a gap of approx. 15cm/6in. in the centre, for filling later. Machine either side of gap.

Clip round the seam allowance at 2.5cm/1in. intervals, either end of the tube.

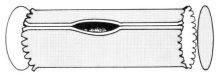

With right sides inside, tack then machine the circular ends to the tube.

Turn the tube right side out, and fill. Close the opening securely with a small ladder stitch.

Make the hard bolster in the same way, but fill it fuller until it feels taut and firm.

Soft bolster cover

REQUIREMENTS

76cm/30in. of 91cm/36in. wide material.
Matching thread, cotton or a synthetic for synthetic fabric.
Pins, scissors.

Cord to draw up each end, available in most furnishing stores. 137cm/1½yds. would be sufficient, a similar colour to your fabric, or a contrast. Make or buy four tassels to attach to the ends. Fold the fabric in half lengthwise, pin or tack together, and machine allowing 13mm/½in. seam allowance. Turn up a 2.5cm/1in. hem either end, turning under 13mm/½in., and machine around each hem, leaving a 2.5cm/1in. gap in each hem to thread the cord through.

Turn right side out and press.

Cut the cord in half, and thread through the hems either end. To thread it through use a large safety pin attached to one end of the cords. Draw one end up, and tie into a bow, insert the cushion into the other end, and draw up similarly. Attach your tassels or bobbles to the four ends.

Hard bolster cover

REQUIREMENTS

91cm/1yd. fabric.
36cm/14in. zip, matching colour.
Sewing thread, matching colour.
Pins, scissors.

Cut a rectangular piece of material 63cm/25in. long, 79cm/31in. wide. Fold in half lengthwise and pin or tack allowing 13mm/½in. seam allowance. Measure 36cm/14in. along the centre, and mark either end with a pin.

Machine seam either side of the pins. Press seam open. Turn right side out.

Lay zip, right side up, under the opening, and tack into position. Machine, using the zipper foot on your machine.

Cut two strips of material 14cm/5½in. long, 79cm/31in. wide. These are for covering either end. Fold in half right sides together, and machine, allowing 13mm/½in. seam allowance. Press seams open. With right sides together, pin each end tube to either end of the main body, as in diagram, machine together on 13mm/½in. seam allowance. Clip around seams at 2.5cm/1in. intervals, and press.

Turn the ends right side out. Gather round both ends, either by hand, or by using the longest stitch on your machine. The first row should be 6mm/¼in. in, the second row 13mm/½in. in from the edge. Draw these stitches up as tightly as possible, so that there is barely a hole seen, pushing the raw edges inside. Tie off securely. Open the zip and insert the cushion. A decorative button can be sewn over the two small holes at either end if desired, or a couple of tassels attached.

A sag bag

These cushion-type chairs, are wonderful fun especially for the youngest members of the family. They are equally useful indoors and

A sag bag surrounded by an assortment of different shaped cushions with piped and fringed edges.

out. They can be used in the nursery, playroom or living room, according to the fabric you choose. They can be biffed and banged, dragged and trodden on, in fact can withstand the hardest of wear if made from suitable fabric like canvas, rexine, soft leather or reinforced sail cloth.

They are filled with polystyrene granules, thus making them very light, and can be moulded into any shape, flat for lying on or upright for sitting.

The shape I find most popular and useful is a rugby-ball shape, made up from six segments of fabric.

REQUIREMENTS

3.20m/3½yds. material, 122cm/48in. wide.
Matching sewing thread (button thread is the strongest, and is available in most furnishing and dress fabric shops).
30cm/12in. sturdy zip (with a lock).
Size 16 needle for the machine. If using a soft leather fabric special leather needles are available at your sewing-machine shop. If they do not have one, contact your nearest machine distributors, and they will send one off for you.
Polystyrene granules 12lbs. (5.5kg), available in 4lb. bags, from any Habitat store, or by mail from Arrowtip Ltd, 31 Stannary St, London SE11.

ASSEMBLING

Make a paper pattern, shaped like an orange segment, 41cm/16in. wide at the centre, and 1.52m/5ft. long. Make the ends slightly rounded, as though you have pushed them in. Lay the fabric out flat, and cut six of your segment shapes, placing them as in the diagram.

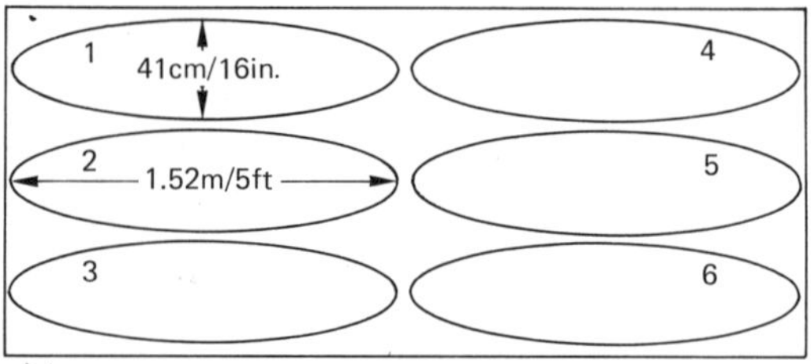

Working with the first three segments, machine the first and third ones to either side of the second, allowing 18cm/¾in. seam allowance.

Machine similarly the fourth and sixth segments to the fifth, making two half rugby-ball shapes.

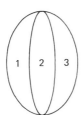 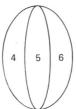

Pin these two halves together, right sides inside, marking a 30cm/12in. gap about 20cm/8in. down from the top of one of the sides. This opening is for the zip, and for filling the bag when completed. Machine down either side, omitting the opening. Turn right side out, and tack the zip into position. Using the zip foot on your machine, stitch into position.

Open the zip, and fill the bag until it is about two-thirds full with the polystyrene granules. Close zip, and place lock into position. If you cannot obtain a zip with a lock, lie the tab flat and stitch down.

Keep any unused granules for topping up later. They tend to compress in use and lose their air after about a year.

These granules can also be used to make a cushion for a pet's basket, in a washable fabric or pvc. They are ideal for dogs or cats as they mould to any shape and are also warm.

Foam block cushions

Pvc-coated fabric will cover foam cushions for the garden and can be left out all the summer, without spoiling. This type of cushion does not need to be piped, or to have a zip. You can buy blocks of foam rubber to any shape or size, ideal for cushions, at most large furnishing stores.

Large foam-filled floor cushions, made from an exotic large print, preferably cotton, are comfortable to relax on. Tabs attached to a foam block-filled cushion can be strung on to a pole, and used in place of a head-board for a bed, or against the wall behind bench-seats.

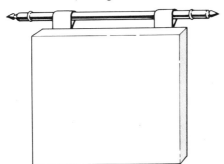

2. Table cloths

As these have to be washed so often, the best fabric to use is a cotton linen mixture, which washes and wears well. Square or rectangular cloths do not need a pattern. A simple hem around the edges of a piece of fabric about 30cm/1ft. larger than the table is sufficient. A round tablecloth can appear complicated, but in fact is quite simple.

Circular tablecloth

Take a tape measure or a long piece of string. Measure from the floor on one side, then up and over the widest part of the table, down to the floor on the opposite side. Adjust the measurement accordingly if you do not want the cloth to reach right down to the floor. This measurement is both the width of your cloth and the length, as it is going to be circular. Most materials are 91cm/36in., 122cm/48in. and 137cm/54in. wide, therefore, as most of your measurements will be over 137cm/54in., there will have to be a join, *not* in the centre where it can easily be seen, but on either side of the overhang.

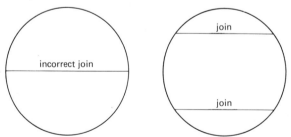

Use newspaper (generally the largest type of paper found in the home), and lay it out on the floor, pinning the pieces together, to the rough length you measured. Allowing 13mm/½in. hem seam, add 2.5cm/1in. to your measurement. Take a drawing pin and attach it

Three quarter length circular tablecloth made from a cotton polyester fabric.

to a piece of string, just over half the length of the tablecloth you have measured. Mark that length with a knot or a pin. Now using the string like a compass place the drawing pin half way along the top edge of the paper, and make the shape of half a circle, onto the paper following the knotted end with a pencil, Cut around your markings and you have your pattern ready.

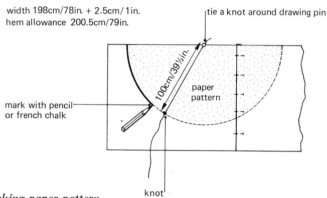

width 198cm/78in. + 2.5cm/1in.
hem allowance 200.5cm/79in.

tie a knot around drawing pin

100cm/39½in.

paper pattern

mark with pencil or french chalk

knot

Making paper pattern

REQUIREMENTS

For a table 81cm/32in. wide, 58cm/23in. high.
3.87m/4¼yds. of 122cm/48in. wide fabric.
Scissors.
Matching sewing thread.
Paper pattern.
6.40m/7yds. fringing or bobbles (optional).

Cutting layout

fold

selvage

1. Fold the material in half, lengthwise, and place your pattern onto it, straight edge on the fold. Cut the overlap off, and place this section, with straight edge to the selvage, alongside, matching patterns if necessary, and allow 13mm/½in. seam allowance. Cut patterns out.

2. Open the main section and pin the two overlap pieces to the selvages, with right sides together, and allowing 13mm/½in. seams.
3. Machine together, and either oversew raw edges, or trim with pinking shears.
4. Press seams open.
5. Hem: (a) Press under 6mm/¼in. all round. Turn up a further 6mm/¼in. and hem either by hand, or machine.
(b) If you are going to add braid, fringing or bobbles, pin the fringing on, when you have completed the hem (a). For a full-length cloth ensure that the base of the fringe is level with the bottom of the hem. Sew on by hand or machine. For a shorter cloth the fringing can be sewn on to the hem seam to allow the fringe to hang beneath the hem line.

Scalloped hem

This type of hem is more accurate and simpler to make if you design and make a template first. Fold the paper pattern you made first in half, and then in half again. Secure the edges with paper clips, to prevent it unfolding. With a pencil, mark the curved edge into equal sections, the size you want the scallops. If the folded curved edge is 76cm/30in. long, and you want small scallops, mark it at 7.5cm/3in. intervals; for larger scallops, mark it 12.5 or 19cm/5 or 7½in. intervals. For the scallops to fit equally all round, the size intervals must divide into your edge length.

Draw around the edge of a cup or plate to make the curve between each interval, making sure you have the same depth between each one.

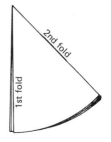
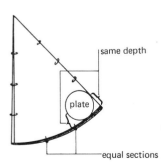

Cut the curves out, thus making your pattern. If you want to keep this pattern for further reference, copy it on to a piece of firm card.

Fold the prepared table cloth in half then into a quarter section, and pin the curved edges together, to prevent them shifting. Pin the paper template on, level with one of the folded sides, draw around the curves with a pencil or french chalk. Unpin the pattern and place level with the other folded side, and repeat.

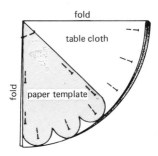

Hem in the same way as shown in section (a) remembering to clip the angles between each scallop.

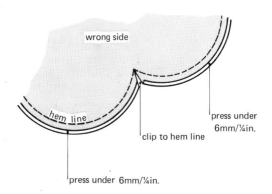

3. Duvets and pillows

Make your own duvet

These continental quilts are warm to use and extremely easy to make. Terylene and cotton sheeting is the best fabric to use, available in most furnishing stores, in 122cm/48in. and 173cm/68in. widths. Synthetic wadding is also available in these stores, or at your local upholstering shop. Down and feather quilts are more difficult and expensive to make.

Allow 23cm/9in. extra overhang each side of the bed. Most beds are 183cm/72in. long unless you have a specially long bed.

Bed size	Duvet size
91cm/3ft.	132cm/4ft.6in.
106cm/3ft. 6in.	152cm/5ft.
122cm/4ft.	168cm./5ft.6in.
132cm/4ft. 6in.	183cm/6ft.
152cm/5ft.	198cm/6ft. 6in.

REQUIREMENTS FOR A 106CM/3FT. 6IN. BED

3.65m/4yds. of 173cm/68in. wide fabric (5.49m/6yds. of 122cm/48in. wide fabric).
1.83m/2yds. of 152cm/60in. wide wadding (4.57m/5yds. of 68cm/27in. wide wadding).
Matching thread, cotton or a synthetic thread.
Tacking thread, pins, needle, a pair of scissors.

Cutting layout

173cm/68in. fabric.

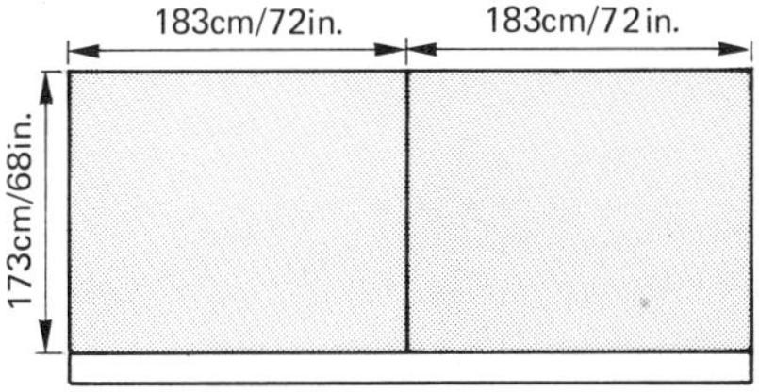

122cm/48in. fabric.

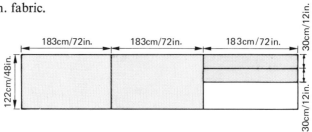

Child's bedroom showing a matching pillow case and lampshade. Also duvet with a variety of pillow cases.

Cut and assemble two rectangles 152 × 183cm/60 × 72in. If using 122cm/48in. wide fabric, machine the extra 30cm/12in. strips, to the 122cm/48in. wide pieces, press open seams.

Pin both rectangles, right sides together, matching corners and centres, machine both sides and across the top.

Turn right side out, press seams.

Lay out flat, and mark across the top and base, with pins, 25cm/10in. gaps. Join these together with either french chalk or pencil lines. You will then be able to follow these when machining wadding and fabric together.

Roll the wadding lengthwise, and put into the prepared cover, starting as near to the side seam as possible, and pushing it well down, to meet the base seam.

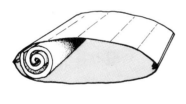 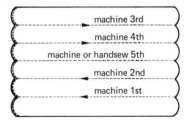

Carefully unroll it, and manoeuvre it until it fits evenly.

Turn under 13mm/½in. along the opening, tack, then machine as near to the edge as possible. A table placed beside your machine will help take the weight of the cover as you are machining.

Using a long tacking thread, tack through the entire cover, following your markings, on all five lines. Then machine the first two outside lines, rolling the cover between the machine on the second seam. Turn the cover round, and machine the opposite two lines similarly. If the cover will roll tight enough, you may be able to machine the centre line, if not, handsew it with small backstitching.

Duvet cover

The best and most crease-resistant fabric to use for bed-linen is Terylene and cotton. This can be obtained in most furnishing stores in 122cm/48in. and 173cm/68in. widths. If you are unable to buy it in the stores around your area, most mills will supply you on request.

REQUIREMENTS

3.65m/4yds. of 173cm/68in. fabric (5.49m/6yds. of 122cm/48in. wide).
Matching sewing thread.
3.65m/4yds. matching tape (13mm/½in. wide).
Cut two matching rectangles 162 × 193cm/64 × 76in. slightly larger than the duvet. Cut as for the duvet, joining the fabric for the 122cm/48in. wide in the same manner.

Place the two rectangles together, right sides inside, matching the corners and sides. Tack together, leaving a 91cm/3ft. opening in the centre of one side.

Machine the three sides, and either side of the opening.

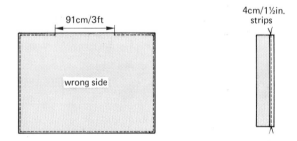

Cut two 4cm/1½in. strips of fabric, 94cm/37in. long. With wrong side facing you, press up 6mm/¼in. on one side of each strip, and machine.

Place each strip, either side of the opening, right sides together, and raw edges together. Turn under the extra 13mm/½in. at either end, and machine on the seam line of the cover.

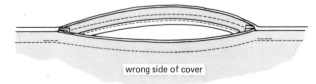

Turn cover right side out, and press. Sew on three 20cm/8in. lengths of tape, space out evenly, on one side of the opening and correspond three more ties on the other side.

Velcro tape could be machined on the two strips instead of tapes. Oversew any raw edges.

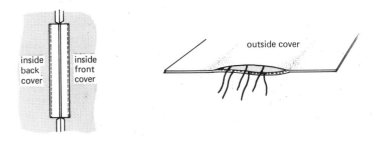

Pillow cases

REQUIREMENTS

To make two; each 48 × 74cm/19 × 29in.
183cm/2yds. fabric 122cm/48in. wide.
Matching cotton.

Fabric layout

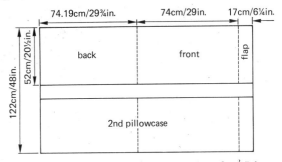

These pillow cases will have french seams, therefore I have allowed 19mm/¾in. seam allowance based on the usual pillow size of 46 × 71cm/18 × 28in. Check with your own pillow before cutting out.

Cut the case in one piece, 166 × 52cm/65½ × 20½in. Turn under 6mm/¼in. either end, and 13mm/½in. again, for hems, machine both ends.

With wrong side facing you, turn over 15cm/6in. at the top, pin together at side on 13mm/½in. seam line. Bring the lower half up level with the top fold, and pin sides at 13mm/½in. seam allowance.

Machine up either side, trim the seams to 6mm/¼in., turn wrong side out, and press seams.

Allowing 6mm/¼in. tack up either side again, and machine.

Turn right side out, and press again.

Method 1

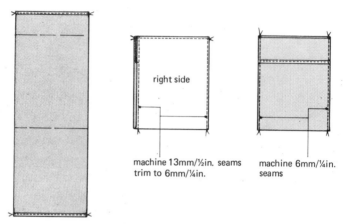

machine 13mm/½in. seams
trim to 6mm/¼in.

machine 6mm/¼in.
seams

Method 2

Machine 19mm/¾in. hems at either end as before. With right side facing you, fold up the lower section C, and fold the flap, A, over C, on fold line. Machine down both sides oversew raw edges. Turn right side out, and press.

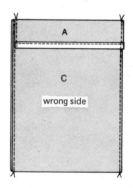

Renewing worn-out feather pillows

Feather pillows cannot be washed and the covers can become very discoloured. Also the fabric eventually wears out. Consequently the feathers begin to come out. Ready-made down-proof covers can

be purchased at most furnishing fabric stores, but you can buy
183cm/2yds. of the light-weight ticking fabric, enough for two
pillow cases, and make the covers.

REQUIREMENTS FOR TWO PILLOW COVERS 48 × 74CM/
19 × 29IN.

183cm/2yds. of down-proof fabric.
Matching thread.

ASSEMBLING

Measure the old pillow across the top lengthwise, and around the
back, adding 2.5cm/1in. for seam allowance. Measure the width
plus 2.5cm/1in. for seams. Cut this rectangular shape out from the
fabric, making the lengthwise measurement lie on the grain of the
fabric.

With right side facing you, fold the fabric up matching the two
narrow ends at the corners, and pin down the two sides. Machine
these two sides, using a small stitch on your machine to prevent the
feathers coming out.

Turn right side out and press seams.

Shake the feathers well down to the bottom in the old case, and
cut carefully across the seam line at the top. Pin these two edges to
the top opening of the new cover, as described on page 11, or tack
them together. Gently shake the feathers from the old case to the
new.

When they are all transferred, pin across the top of the new case,
about 5cm/2in. down, to prevent the feathers from flying out as you
remove the tacking or pins.

Turn under 13mm/½in. along the top edge, and machine a double
row of stitches, as near the edge as possible.

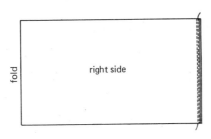

4. Loose covers

A 'loose cover' does not mean that it should be loose and sloppy looking. When completed, it should look and fit like an upholstered or fitted cover. Generally the seams are piped, which not only gives it a professional finish, but longer wear.

Choose your fabric wisely, to compliment your surroundings, matching it with the curtains or carpet. If the carpet is plain, use a patterned fabric and vice versa. It can look effective to use a contrasting fabric for the piping.

The type of fabric should be chosen carefully. Avoid loose woven fabrics, velvets and velours, light-weight cottons which wear out quickly, and any material which is likely to shrink a lot after the first wash. Most cottons shrink about 2% if dry cleaned, and 5% if hand or machine washed.

Remember that patterned fabrics always need more material, because patterns have to be matched, and some wastage must be expected. I would suggest a cotton union is the best fabric to choose, as it is both hard-wearing and washes well with very little shrinkage.

If this is your first cover I would suggest you use either a plain fabric or one that has an overall small design, where you will have no pattern matching. Choose a simple chair first. A small bedroom chair without wings make a good start. Even simpler, you could try a stool which requires just a seat, side strip and valance.

The secrets of success lie in the accuracy of measuring for the least amount of wastage, and the accuracy of your cutting and assembling. This is easier if you make paper patterns first.

Preparing the patterns

Study the chair carefully, and estimate how many patterns you are going to require. If the chair has an old cover you can estimate from that, but do not make patterns from it, as some of the parts which may have covered a curve and therefore have had some stress put on them, will have been pulled out of shape, giving you an inaccurate shape to follow. Follow the seams in the existing chair. These seams will also indicate where most of your piping will come.

You will notice that the fabric on the existing chair has threads going vertically and horizontally. These threads are known as the *weft*, which runs crosswise or selvage to selvage, and the *warp*, which runs lengthwise or up and down. The *warp* thread is always the stronger and is termed as the 'grain' of the fabric.

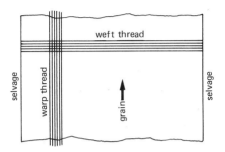

Measure the longest and widest parts of each section, adding 19mm/¾in. for *all* seams. Cut a piece of paper to the size you have measured, which will be a rectangular shape, and pin it to the chair with a couple of pins, to check that the horizontal and vertical shape of your pattern corresponds with the 'weft' and 'warp' threads of the chair. As most chairs tilt back, the outside arm sections look rather like a 'squashed' rectangle, but the grain must always run horizontal, as shown in the diagram.

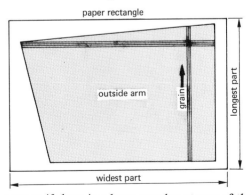

Trim the pattern if there is a large surplus at any of the sides, but do not pin or cut any darts or curves. These will be more accurately made when you are assembling the pieces of fabric.

Decide how you are going to finish the base: for instance you could have a valance or frill, you could show the legs of the chair and finish off with a piped edge, or you could join the edges underneath with tape.

Calculating the amount of material – trimmings

INVERTED PLEATS FOR THE VALANCE

Place a pin at each corner of the chair, at the height of the valance, tie a piece of string around the pins for reference when measuring the lengths required for the outside arms, back and front seat panel.

Measure the total around the string. Add 20cm/8in. at each corner for the inverted pleats.

> i.e. Total length 305cm/120in.
> 4 20cm/8in. pleats 81cm/32in.
> Length required 386cm/152in.

For a 20cm/8in. deep valance, add 4cm/1½in. for the hem, and 18mm/¾in. for the top seam allowance. This will equal 25.8cm/10¼in.

As most fabrics are 122–137cm/48–54in. wide, divide the total length by 122cm/48in. (width of the fabric). 386cm/152in. divided by 122cm/48in. equals 3, plus 20cm/8in. You now know that you need 3 strips of fabric 25.8cm/10¼in. deep, plus an extra strip 20cm/8in. long by 25.8cm/10¼in. deep. Allow 104cm/41in., the remaining part of the short strip can be used up for piping, or for the cushion side-strips.

PLEATED ALL ROUND OR BOX PLEATS

Measure the length around the valance line, and according to the size of the pleats, allow two or two and a half times that length. Having found the total length, divide this by 122cm/48in. and multiply the result by the depth of the valance.

GATHERED FRILL

Measure the length around the frill line, and allow one and a half times that length. Estimate the amount required as for the other types of valances.

Wing chair with loose cover, showing piped seams and a box-pleat valance.

PIPED AROUND BASE

Allow 19mm/¾in. seam allowance on the back, outside arms, and front sections.

JOINED UNDERNEATH WITH TAPE

Allow 10cm/4in. extra on back, outside arms and front panel sections.

If it is a wing chair, feel up the sides of the wings, to determine the amount of extra material that will be required to 'tuck in'. Also feel around the seat, as most chairs have 'tuck-ins', or room for the fabric to be tucked in, with the advantage of being able to pull the cover taut and to keep it in position, thus avoiding too much creasing after being sat upon. Allow an extra 10cm/4in. at the base of the front, both inside arms, the back and two sides of the seat sections.

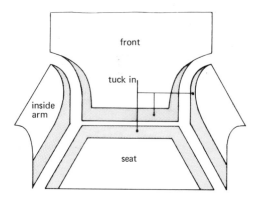

As you make each pattern, make sure that all the lengthwise measurements are indicated on the paper by an arrow, to prevent a pattern being cut out upside-down. Name each section and the number required e.g. BACK 1, OUTSIDE ARM 2; this will prevent any confusion when calculating the amount of fabric required, and in cutting out.

Calculating the amount of fabric required for the piping can be difficult. If you estimate 46cm/18in. of 122cm/48in. fabric will make 10–10.97m/11–12yds. of piping, 91cm/36in. of fabric should be more than enough for an armchair, with one separate seat cushion.

When you have measured, cut and marked every section, lay them out on the floor with all the arrows showing the grain, pointing in the same direction, placing them no wider than 122cm/48in., (width of fabric), as shown in this example.

Measure the total combined length to calculate how much material you need, not forgetting to add extra for the piping. Any spare material can always be utilized for piping, or facings for the opening.

If you are using a patterned fabric, place a cross on the paper patterns where the centre of a pattern is to come, so as to correspond and match the patterns on either side of the chair. The most notice-able parts for pattern matching are the front section and inside arms, the top of the cushion, and the front of the valance. It is not essential for the sides or back to match, as they are rarely seen together, unless the backs of the chairs are facing the door.

POINTS TO REMEMBER

Patterned fabrics need extra material, for matching.
Allow 91cm/36in. extra per chair for piping strips.
When buying the cord, make sure it has been pre-shrunk. If it has not, purchase at least 25% more, to allow for the shrinkage when you wash it, before use.

REQUIREMENTS OTHER THAN THE FABRIC

18.28–22.86m/20–25yds. piping cord No. 4 (unless material is very thick, then use No. 3).
Matching sewing thread, preferably Drima or a synthetic as it is stronger, and longer wearing.
2 zips, velcro, or popper-tape, approx. 46–51cm/18–20in. long. One for the cover opening, the other for the cushion.
Hook and eye, medium size.
Tacking thread.
Pins, a needle, scissors – one large pair for cutting out and one small pair.

Assembling

Mark the centre line of your chair from the top of the front, down the centre of the seat, to the valance level with pins. This will help to centralize a patterned fabric, and act as a guide for the warp or lengthwise grain of the fabric.

Lay the fabric out smoothly, having ironed out any deep creases beforehand. Place your paper patterns on the fabric, matching any patterns, and following the grain of the fabric carefully.

Cut the front piece out first, then the inside arms (and inside wings, if a wing chair). Pin the front section, wrong side out, on the chair, making sure that the fabric is central, smoothing it out from the centre. Place the pins on the chair seam lines, and cut away the excess material, leaving 18mm/¾in. overlap for the seams. Cut the curves out at the arms, remembering to leave enough for any tuck-in there may be. If the corners on the top seam are very rounded, you may have to pin a couple of darts each side.

For a wing chair, place the inside wing sections next, wrong side out, placing a couple of pins in the centre to hold the section in place, with the grain correct. Smooth out from the centre, again pinning on the chair seam lines. According to how curved the wings are, you will have to make darts in the same positions evenly spaced on either side with pins.

Pin the inside straight sides to the front section, allowing enough for the tuck-ins, equally both sides.

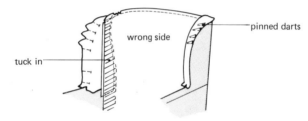

Place the inside arms, wrong side out again, into position making sure that there is enough fabric to attach to the front panel for any tuck-in. Allow these arm sections to overlap the front of the arms by 19mm/¾in. for joining onto the front arm scrolls later.

Cut the armhole curve out, to correspond with the inside wing section (if a wing chair), or to correspond with the front section, as shown in the diagram.

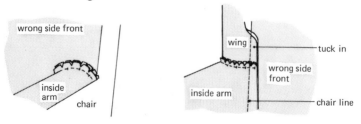

Pin together, clipping the curve and trimming to the seam allowance. This curve is very acute, and you will find that you must clip towards the seam at 13mm/½in. intervals to enable the seam to lie flat. Machine this seam carefully. It is not piped, trim to 13mm/½in. and oversew the raw edges. For a wing chair, machine this seam first, before joining to the front section.

You may find it easier to fold the front panel in half, pinning it to the chair with the fold following the centre pin line. You then cut the shape of the armholes, both sides at once. The only disadvantage in doing it this way is that some chairs are not identical either side, especially if they are rather old ones. Remember when cutting away the excess material that you can never replace material cut off, but a seam can always be made smaller. Be extra generous with your seam allowance. It can always be trimmed down afterwards.

The inside of the chair is now completed, except for the seat. This you assemble later.

Prepare at least 9.14m/10yds. of piping now, from the oddments, or 46cm/18in. of the material.

For a wing chair, fit and trim the outside wing sections, and tack the piping around the front curve only. Pin these sections to the prepared cover, and machine.

For both types of chairs fit the outer arm sections, wrong side out, insert the piping along the top seam, tack, and then machine.

Fit and cut to shape the two front scrolls, matching them as evenly as possible. Ensure the scrolls are long enough to meet the valance line, plus seam allowance. Pipe around them, omitting the base seam. Pin into position, wrong side out, pinning the excess material of the arms into evenly spaced darts if the scrolls are smaller in

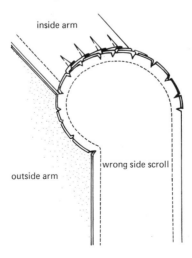

inside arm

wrong side scroll

outside arm

circumference than the arms. Machine into position, with the darts pressed upwards. It is not necessary to machine each individual dart, the machined seam line is sufficient. Trim the seams, clip around the curves, and oversew raw edges.

Pipe around the two sides and top of the front seat panel, with tacking stitches, and attach to the seat section leaving 19mm/¾in. open at either end, for joining to the bottom of the inside arms, as shown in the diagram A and B.

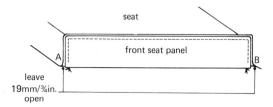

Join the seat to the base of the inside arms and front panel.

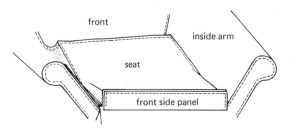

Measure and cut the amount of piping required for going around the top and two sides of the back. Tack into position, leaving the zip opening free. The free piece of piping will be attached to the adjacent side when you stitch them together.

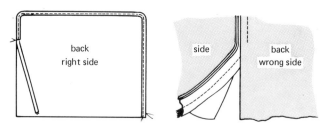

Pin the back into position, clipping any curves, and pinning the extra piping to the adjacent side. Machine and finish off.

Openings

The openings can be finished off with hooks and eyes (size 3 is preferable), a zip, velcro, or popper-tape, obtainable at most furnishing stores, to any length required; generally 46 to 51cm/18 to 20in.

HOOKS AND EYES

Cut a 7.5cm/3in. strip of material 13mm/½in. longer than opening. Fold in half lengthwise, and crease. Allowing 13mm/½in. seams on this strip, encase and machine onto the seam line of the back section, placing the strip 13mm/½in. above the top of the opening.

Cut a 5cm/2in. strip of the same length of material and machine under 6mm/¼in. down one side. With right sides together, place the strip on the other side of the opening, leaving 13mm/½in. excess at the top, and machine. Turn the strip in, and press. Handsew the two strips together, across the top, and finish off the raw edges.

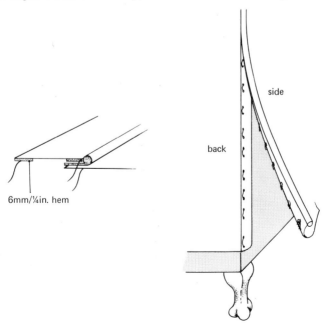

6mm/¼in. hem

side

back

VELCRO OPENING

Finish the opening as for the hooks and eyes. Machine the velcro onto either side, placing a hook and eye at the base, above the piping line.

ZIP OPENING

Tack one side of the zip as close to the piping seam as possible, Press the seam line of the other side of the opening and tack zip into position. Handsew or machine zip and finish off the raw edges. A hook and eye can be sewn at the base to prevent the zip from opening on stress.

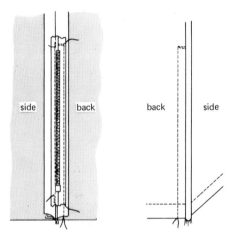

Tack the piping for the valance around the cover at the required height for the valance. Cut the required number of strips, allowing 20cm/8in. for each corner, for the inverted pleats. Machine these together, remembering to centralize the front strip, both for pattern matching, and to prevent any seams showing. Ensure all strips are the right way up.

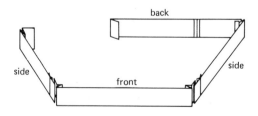

Turn up 4cm/1½in. hem, turn under 13mm/½in., and machine. Finish the two ends similarly.

Tack into position along the piping, allowing 5cm/2in. excess at one end and 15cm/6in. at the other. Fold the inverted pleats at each corner, with the 20cm/8in. allowed, tacking across the top and bottom to secure, leaving the excess material free at the opening corner.

Wrap the 5cm/2in. excess around the edge, and machine the valance into position. Do not wrap the extra 15cm/6in. around, but leave this end free.

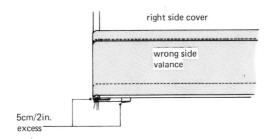

With the valance hanging down in the finished position, pleat the excess 15cm/6in., allowing 5cm/2in. at the end. Handsew into place. Sew two hooks at the top of the excess 5cm/2in., and the eyes on the inside of the other corner. Press the pleats, remove tacking, finish off any raw edges.

Double-piped cushion

Pipe around both top and bottom of the seat pieces. Cut the side strips to the required length, and join together. Press seams open and oversew any raw edges.

Tack the strip onto the top section of the cushion, machine, and finish off.

Mark either end of the opening for the zip on the bottom section with pins, then tack it onto the other side of the strip, ensuring the

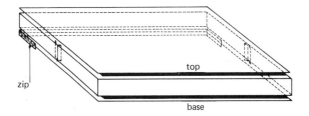

opening is at the back. Machine into place, omitting the opening. Remove tacking, trim seam, and clip the corners.

Turn right side out, and insert the zip either by hand or machine. Finish off any raw edges.

Settee

The idea of making a settee cover may alarm you, but when you have managed the chair cover, you will realize that a settee is just an elongated chair. If it is a three-piece suite you are covering, the shape of the arms and the height will be the same. Here is a simplified sketch.

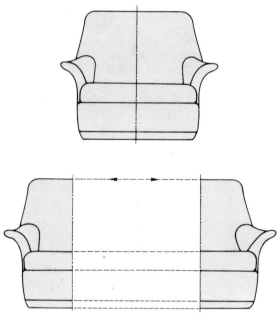

By following the chair instructions, section by section, first machine the vertical lines pressing open the seams, as you reach each stage (these seams are not piped). Do not forget to match patterns.

An extra inverted pleat can be added, in the centre of the valance, at the front, according to your taste.

Finishing the base of a loose cover

There are several possibilities:

1. Valance.

Inverted pleats at each corner.

Pleated all around.

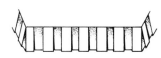

Gathered all around.

2. Piped around the base, backed with a facing strip, sewn onto the inside.

3. Joined underneath with tape, slotted through the hem.

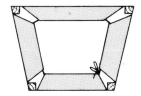

JOINED UNDERNEATH WITH TAPE

Having completed the cover, mark the position of the top of the legs with pins or a pencil, 2.5cm/1in. lower. Cut the excess material away. Cut a strip 2.5cm/1in. wide, on the cross, and machine across the cut line, allowing 13mm/½in. seams. Trim the seams to 6mm/¼in., clip the corners, and press under. Turn under and hem the lower edges, allowing enough width to slot the tape through.

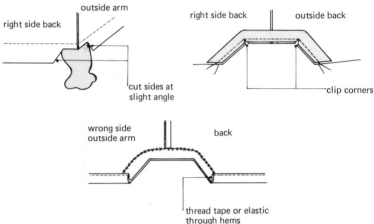

Extra arm caps

If the chair is in constant use, the top of the arms are the first places to become worn. There is generally enough spare material to make a small pair of arm caps.

Make a pattern the same design as the chair cover, about three-quarters the width of the arm, and long enough to be able to be tucked inside the cushion. (If you do not have enough material for that length, they can be shorter.) Use just the top of the scroll pattern, allowing 13mm/½in. for a hem at the bottom.

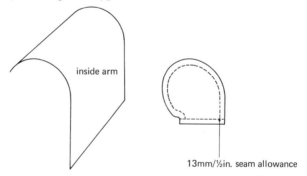

Machine a small hem across the base of the scroll. Pipe around the rest of the scroll.

Machine a small hem across the top, down one side, and across the base of the inside arm piece.

Starting at the outside of the scroll, pin it to the raw edge of the inside arm section, allowing 13mm/½in. seam. Machine into position.

Turn under the remainder of the raw edge of the inside arm, allowing 13mm/½in., clip at the base of the scroll, and machine the remainder of the hem.

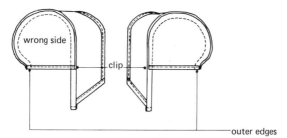

Remember that each scroll is different. The outside of one begins on the left-hand side, and the outside of the other begins on the right-hand side.

Special clear (transparent) buttons, with screws on one side for screwing into the chair to prevent the corners of the arm caps flying out, can be purchased at any large store.

5. Lampshades

To show you how to make every type of lampshade could take a whole book, as there are so many varieties. I have chosen a few of the most popular, which you can then vary, according to your taste.

Lampshades can be made to almost any shape or size. They can be a prominent feature in each room, or they can be made to blend, by the subtle colours chosen. As long as the bulb is not in contact with the shade, the majority of fabrics can be used in safety.

Most soft shades are best if they are lined, especially if they are made from fabrics like voile, chiffon or a fine cotton. This gives the shade a more professional finish, and also covers the struts of the frame.

There are many possibilities for covering materials besides fabric. For instance wallpaper, buckram, parchment, string, raffia, plastic ribbon and many more.

If you are going to choose a cotton fabric on a lined shade, choose a cotton lining, like poplin or fine lawn cotton. Shantung and satin crêpes are most effective on bowed frames, as they stretch more easily. Lace on top of a sateen-backed crêpe, sateen side up looks very pretty and feminine, ideal for a bedroom.

White linings always give a much brighter light. Blues and greens give a cool look, pinks and peachy colours a warm effect, and yellows a bright sunny effect.

Always use a sharp pair of scissors. Preferably keep two pairs – a large pair for cutting out the fabric, and a small pair for the trimming. Steel pins or the glass-headed pins are the best to use, and short needles (Sharp's), are the best for stitching the fabrics. Always use a thimble, otherwise your fingers will suffer. All these items can be purchased at most needlework or craft shops, where you can also buy your frame. Choose the frame carefully. Make sure it is not bent, and that there are no sharp ends left sticking out. These can always be smoothed off with a file at home.

An assortment of lampshades showing different sizes and designs.

Half-globe lampshade

One of the simplest types of shade is a half-globe – ideal for a child's bedroom or the bathroom. It is easily made from a short rectangular piece of fabric, maybe left over from the curtains of that room. There is no need to bind this frame, but it is advisable to paint it with a good gloss paint, preferably the colour of the fabric you have chosen. This makes the frame less visible when looking up into it, and will prevent it from rusting, especially if it is in the humid atmosphere of a bathroom.

MEASURING

Measure the base circle, and add as much again. Measure the length of one of the struts, and add 15cm/6in. for the frill and turnings.

This shade cover is cut on the straight grain of the fabric, and is suitable for most types of fabric, especially cottons.

REQUIREMENTS

Half-globe frame.
Approximately 46cm/18in. of fabric.
Matching thread, a cotton or synthetic.
Elastic 6mm/¼in. wide, the length of the bottom ring of the shade.
Tape 6mm/¼in. wide, 30cm/12in.
Pins, a needle (Crewel) and scissors.
Gloss paint, for painting the frame.
Cut out the rectangular pattern you have measured, and lay it down with the wrong side uppermost.

Turn over 19mm/¾in. along the top edge, tuck under 6mm/¼in. and tack. Turn up 13mm/½in. along the bottom edge, tuck under 6mm/¼in. and tack. Machine along both these edges, then remove the tacking.

Any lace or trimmings you want around the hem should be stitched on now.

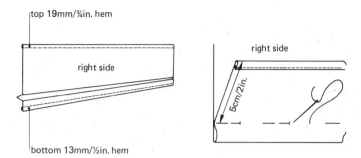

top 19mm/¾in. hem

right side

right side

5cm/2in.

bottom 13mm/½in. hem

Lay cover wrong side uppermost again, and measure 5cm/2in. above hem line, mark with pins at 10cm/4in. intervals. Measure a further 19mm/¾in. above the previous pins, and again mark with pins. With right side facing, fold the hem up until the pins are level with each other. Tack along this line, removing the pins as you stitch.

Machine along this tacking line, and remove tacking. This tuck is for threading the elastic through.

Cut a piece of narrow elastic, 5cm/2in. shorter the the measurement of the bottom ring of the frame. Sew one end to the edge of the tuck, thread it through, drawing up the material, and secure by oversewing to the other edge.

Fold the cover in half, *wrong* sides together, joining the side seams, and machine a seam, 13mm/½in. wide, leaving the top hem free. Clip just below the top hem to the seam line, and cut along the seam line across the hem to remove the corner. Trim the rest of the seam 6mm/¼in.

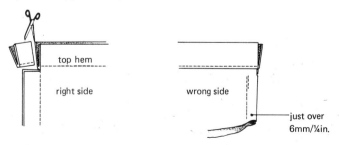

top hem

right side

wrong side

just over 6mm/¼in.

Turn wrong side out and press seam. Tack along the seam again, just over 6mm/¼in., and machine, again leaving the top hem free. Turn right side out and press seam.

Thread a narrow piece of tape through the top hem, and draw the fabric up to the size of the top ring. Secure each end of the tape to the ends of the hem, with a pin, and machine along the seam line, over the tapes.

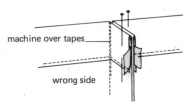

machine over tapes

wrong side

The cover is now completed and just has to be slipped over the frame, adjusting the gathers so that they lie evenly.

Lined lampshade, empire style

This style shade can be made from most fabrics, but is ideal for fine cottons and chiffons. The frame should be covered in a loose weave tape first, on which the lining and outer cover will be sewn. The tape can be bought in most needlework shops. You can use bias binding if you open out one side, but the other special loose weave tape is cheaper and is made especially for the job.

Standard lamp shade, empire style, made from cotton sateen.

The frame can also be painted first, with a good gloss paint, to prevent it from rusting when washed.

REQUIREMENTS

Empire shaped frame.
46cm/18in. material for shades up to 25cm/10in. in diameter, 69cm/27in. for 30cm/12in. shades, and 91cm/36in. for standard shades.
Same amount of fabric for the lining.
Matching thread for both fabrics, cotton or Sylko.
Steel pins, Sharp's No. 9 needle, or a short fine one.
Tape for binding.
Sharp pair of scissors.

BINDING THE FRAME

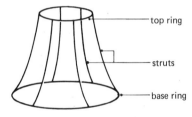

Cover all the struts first, except one, starting at the top of each one and working down. The last strut is bound in one operation with the top and bottom rings.

Measure a strut, and cut a piece of tape 3 times longer than measurement.

Hold one end of the tape at the top of a strut, and in front. Pass the tape up and over the top ring, down behind, and bring out on the left side of the strut, over the end you are holding, working around the strut left to right. Pull taught after each turn, covering a quarter of the previous turn, and keep as smooth and uniform as possible. Should you have to stop, secure it with a pin to prevent it un-ravelling.

When you reach the bottom ring, pass the tape behind the strut, hold firmly with a finger while you pass it under the ring, and up around the strut again. Pass the tape under the front loop and pull taut as you remove your finger from the back. This forms a secure enough knot, until you cover it, when you bind the lower ring. Cut the tape, leaving about 13mm/½in. spare.

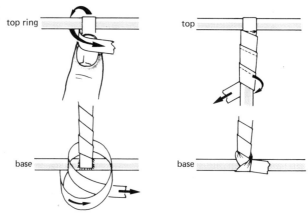

Bind all the struts except one similarly. Measure the top ring, last strut, and bottom ring. Cut a length of tape twice that length, to ensure that you do not run short at the last moment. Should you have to make a join in the tape, secure the bound tape with a pin while you turn under 13mm/½in. and sew the new piece over the last 13mm/½in. Any bumps in the binding should be avoided at all costs, as they will show through, when the light is switched on. The binding *must* be really taut. Otherwise the lining and cover may move out of alignment since they have to be stretched on very smoothly.

Starting at the last strut, hold the end of the tape in front and at the top of the last strut on the upper ring. Pass the tape over the ring, working left to right, down behind and come out on the left side of the strut. Pass it over the end you are holding, and continue working along the ring, making a figure of eight at the top of each strut.

Having completed the ring, and arrived back at the strut, with the tape at the front, pass it over the top ring, just covering the first knot, down the back, and come out on the left side of the last strut. Continue down as before and around the base ring, as you have done with the top ring.

At the finish, secure with a pin, turn under the raw edge, after trimming it to within 13mm/½in., and neatly sew it to the taped frame.

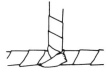

PATTERN FOR LINING AND COVER

For a shade with bowed struts it is easier to cut the fabric on the bias (or 'cross') of the fabric, as you will find that it stretches and lies flatter on the curves, giving a more professional finish.

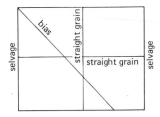 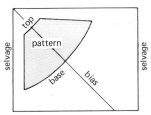

Normally 91cm/36in. of fabric is sufficient for a standard lampshade, and 46cm/18in. for a 25–30cm/10–12in. wide shade. To find a rough idea of the amount of material you will need, make a quick paper pattern, as follows.

Lie the frame on a sheet of paper. With a pencil, mark the centre of the top ring, and centre point of the base ring. Roll it carefully to the left, marking the lines of the top and base rings, and down the strut at the half way point. Roll it back to the right and mark similarly. This will give you a rough pattern of half of the frame.

Cut the pattern out, and with a ruler and pencil join the top and bottom centre marks. This is the true bias line, as shown in the diagram, which enables the fabric to stretch evenly and prevent it

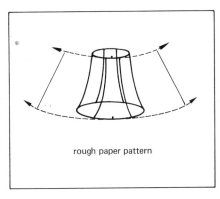

rough paper pattern

puckering. This pattern is sufficient for both lining and cover, as the difference between the two is only 3mm/⅛in.

Fold the fabric on the bias, and pin the sides together. Using large tacking stitches, tack both sides and the fold together and remove pins.

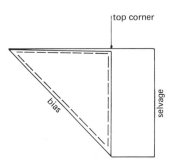

With the top corner uppermost, place the fabric on the frame, adjusting it to cover half the framework. Pin the fabric to the centre of the top ring. Use steel pins or glass-headed pins. Pull the fabric gently down, and place a pin in the centre of the base ring. Continue pulling the fabric away from the centre pin either side, and place more pins at the base of each strut and in between.

Having finished the base ring, stretch the fabric upwards and outwards, and place two more pins at the top of the outside struts. The centre pin on the top ring may need adjusting. Do this now before pinning the side struts.

Pin down the sides. Remembering that the material is on the bias, so any wrinkles that appear between the side pins can be removed by following the grain of the fabric to the base ring, and altering the pin there. When you have completed the sides by pinning at about 2.5cm/1in. intervals, complete the top ring. The fabric should now be taut and smooth. Cut away the excess material, leaving at least 5cm/2in. all round, and cut the sides if the fabric is rather tight, to within 2.5cm/1in. of the struts.

Remove the pins one by one, unpinning them from the frame, but repinning the fabric again.

It is difficult to pin both the lining and the cover material on together, but using the pattern of your cover for the lining can also be inaccurate, because the fabric stretches. You must therefore repeat the same procedure with the lining material to get it really accurate.

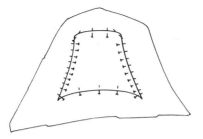

SEWING ON THE COVER

Tack the two sides following your pins, removing them as you stitch. Machine. Remove tacking and trim the seams to about two-tenths of an inch, and press open.

Slide the cover over the frame, pinning the top strut pins and side ones first. Make sure the seams lie over the side struts by pinning them top and bottom. Continue pinning around the top ring and base ring, with pins close together. Using double thread oversew the cover onto the bound frame, with small, close-together stitches.

If the material is fine, trim the seams to 13mm/½in., turn up over your stitching, and oversew again, trimming the material just above your stitches. If the material is strong and does not fray too much, there is no need to oversew again, but trim the edge as near to the stitching as you can to avoid it fraying off.

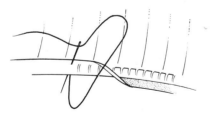

SEWING ON THE LINING

Machine your side seams 3mm/⅛in. inside the pin line, as this is slightly smaller than the cover. Trim and press the seams as before. Place the frame upside down, and put the lining inside. With the seams facing you, pin the top and bottom of the seams first, and then the struts in between them next. The base will be no trouble to pin, but the light fitting, or gimbal, at the top will prevent the lining from lying smoothly.

Cut the surplus material carefully, down to the level of the gimbal, then stretch the fabric towards the ring again, so that there are no wrinkles left. Overlap the slashed edges, turning under the edge of the top edge. Oversew the lining on to the frame as you did for the cover, stitching right through to the tape. This can be hard on the fingers, so use a thimble, otherwise your fingers will suffer.

Cut the extra material off as close as possible. Cut a couple of strips of the extra lining fabric, about 2.5cm/1in. wide, 5cm/2in. long, fold and place on the top ring, and sew onto the ring around the gimbal. This is not always necessary, but will give the shade a more professional finish. You can now add your braid or trimmings around the top and base rings, either by handsewing, or by sticking with a fabric glue like Copydex, or Uhu.

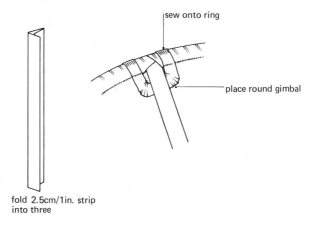

sew onto ring

place round gimbal

fold 2.5cm/1in. strip into three

Drum lampshade

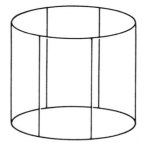

This type of shade can be made up from almost any material but particularly lends itself to parchment, backed wallpaper, buckram or any rigid material. For a small wall-light shade iron-on Vilene is sufficient for a backing for most soft fabrics and wallpaper. But larger frames need a firmer backing like buckram. This is obtainable in several thicknesses, at most furnishing stores, or your local upholsterer.

Make a pattern first from a piece of firm card. Tie a piece of cotton, or use chalk to mark one of the struts on the frame.

Place the frame on the card, and draw down the side of the marked strut. Roll the frame carefully across the card, marking the top and bottom rings, until you reach the marked strut. Allow an extra 13mm/½in. for joining the seams.

Cut the rectangular pattern out, and fit around the frame, using clothes pegs for securing it. Make sure that it fits correctly.

Cut out your fabric and backing material. Using a hot iron, press the backing evenly onto the fabric. Always start from the centre and work towards the edges. This will prevent puckering and air bubbles. Any imperfections like this will show up more when the light is switched on.

Fit the fabric around the frame, securing with the clothes pegs as before. Stick the seam together with fabric glue, and press together firmly with your fingers.

Cut two pieces of wide braid the length of the rings, and glue around the edges, turning half of it to the back of the frame, enclosing the ring.

If you wish to sew the fabric on, you must cover the frame first with tape. Cut the tape 2.5cm/1in. longer than the ring. Place it lengthwise along the ring, and oversew the edges as firmly as possible. Turn under the last edge 6mm/¼in. to overlap the beginning, and oversew together.

Stab stitch the cover to the frame, as shown in the diagram.

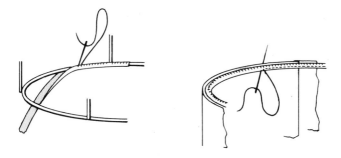

6. Drop seat chair cover

Renewing a drop seat chair cover borders on upholstery, but I have included this as it is very simple to do, and cuts out the high labour costs. It is only worth doing if the seat is undamaged and the webbing underneath is intact. If some of the webbing is broken, the wadding will have to be removed and the hessian under it, and this then involves using special upholstery tools, which are quite expensive just for one small job. A local upholsterer will repair it for you, leaving you just to re-cover it.

Remove the old cover carefully, using either a tack lifter or a screw-driver and hammer, making sure you do not damage the wood. If you have a tack lifter, place the head under the tack, and gently lever out. Using a screw-driver, place the head of the screw-driver under the head of the tack, hammer gently, in the direction of the grain of the wood to prevent it splitting, and lever the tack out.

If the seat has been covered many times before and there are old tacks still left in, remove these also, as they may be in a position where you will need to tack. These holes can always be filled with plastic wood, obtainable in tubes at most do-it-yourself shops, or some furnishing stores, which will reinforce the wood for further tacks to be put in.

This is also a good time to check for wood worm, especially if it is an old chair. Rentokil do a large range of insecticide sprays and solutions for painting on, and will give you further information on how to prevent woodworm. The tell-tale marks of the woodworm are small pin-head holes in the wood.

Use the old cover as a pattern. If it is too badly damaged use an old piece of muslin or material that you can pull the thread from, to use as a guide-line to find the horizontal and vertical lines. It is essential that the grain runs perfectly true from the back to the front of the seat. This prevents the fabric stretching out of shape when applying it.

Cut the muslin larger than the seat, and pull out the centre

Drop seat chair using a regency striped cotton sateen.

horizontal and vertical threads. If using another fabric, draw the lines with a pencil following the threads across.

Draw similar lines on the seat. Placing the muslin on the seat, match the centre first, and work outwards. Allow enough extra at the sides to fold over and under the seat, and to be able to turn under at least 2.5cm/1in. on the underside.

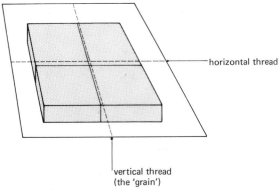

horizontal thread

vertical thread
(the 'grain')

Drawing the lines on the chair seat will aid you when you put in the first tacks.

Place the pattern on your fabric, again matching the horizontal and vertical threads, and cut out. There is no need to cut the excess out at the corners yet, this can be done later.

Place the seat into the centre of your fabric, ensuring that the grain is on the straight.

Starting at the centre back fold the fabric over the sides, turn under the raw edge, and place the first tack in. Do not hammer it completely home yet, in case you need to alter it later.

Do the same with the front side, pulling the fabric over gently to make it taut. Place two more tacks either side. At the same time ease the fabric outwards and over. Keep checking that the horizontal and vertical lines are even.

Work the two sides similarly, again starting at the centre. Continue placing the tacks at 3.8–5cm/1½–2in. intervals, working from the centre, outwards, to within 7.5cm/3in. of the corners.

Corners

Pull the corner fabric taut, up and over the centre of the corner. Place one tack in. Do the same with the opposite corner, checking that the fabric is still central. Do similarly with the other two corners.

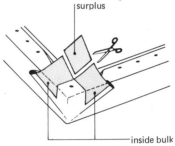

Cut the surplus material away, as shown in the diagram. Fold the material either side of the corner, tucking the bulk inside. Turn under the raw edges and tack down. If you are using thicker material than the original cover, cut away the inside bulk, leaving just enough to turn under.

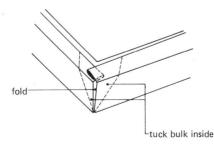

When the seat is finished, cut a piece of hessian or oil-cloth, the same size as the base of the seat. Turn the raw edges under, and tack onto the underside of the seat, covering the webbing and previous tacks. Pull it taut as you go round, starting at the centre back, and centre front. Continue around the seat putting the tacks in, in the same order as for the seat.

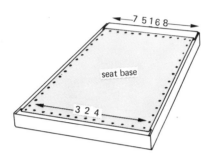

7. Curtains

The most essential part of success in making curtains is to have the correct measurements. Too little material could cause failure, and too much, a waste of money. They are very simple to make, providing you have a large working surface, either the dining-room table, or a large floor space, which can be kept clear for a short while. No special tools are required, just a sewing machine, pins, a fine Crewel needle, a large pair of scissors for cutting the fabric, and a small pair for the sewing threads.

There are many types of curtains, and a wide variety of headings. Linings come in a variety of colours, and not only protect the fabric from the sunlight to prevent discolouration, but also add body to the curtain. A milium lining, which is backed in silver, helps to insulate the room when they are drawn. Another good insulating material, for a cold room, is interlining. This is rather like a fine blanket and is placed between the curtain fabric and the lining. Silks and fine cottons look exceptionally thick and plush worked this way.

Synthetic materials like Acrilan, Courtelle, glass fibre and Dralon wash easily and are practically shrink-proof and sun-resistant. Sheer, semi-sheer and loose woven fabrics are not generally lined, to enable them to give a soft diffusion of light. Detachable linings can be made for use during the winter months, for insulation. Coloured linings can look very effective, from both outside and in, on a white or cream coloured sheer fabric.

Types of headings

Determining the type of heading for your curtains depends on several factors: the type of track, the amount of fabric, whether you have a pelmet, and the effect you want to give.

Full length velour curtains with the heading covering the curtain track.

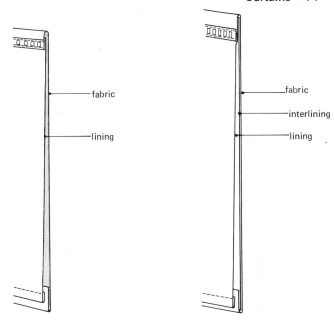

side view of lined curtain   side view interlined curtain

HEADING UNDER A PELMET

As these headings are not seen, Rufflette tape is the best to use. You will only need one and a half times the length of your track, of fabric, against 2–2½ times the length for other more elaborate headings.

This tape is simple to sew on, and needs no special hooks for hanging.

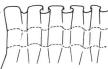

HEADINGS FOR WINDOWS WITH NO PELMET

The simplest and most effective tape to use is Regis tape. This will give the curtains a 7.5–10cm/3–4in. deep heading, according to how far from the top you sew it. It is sewn on exactly the same as the Rufflette tape, and drawn up in the same way. It is suitable for any type of material, and track. It can be sewn on reversed, to hang under a pole, and requires no special hooks.

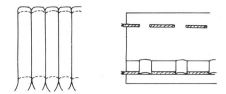

For sheer, semi-sheer fabrics, and net curtains, Tervoil tape will give the same effect as the Regis tape.

Trident tape also gives the same effect, but has the advantage of three levels for the hooks.

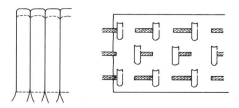

Evenpleat tape will give small pencil pleats, similar to the regis tape.

All these tapes need more fabric, at least twice the length of the track to give the heading its proper effect, and to allow the pencil pleats to lie evenly.

DEEP-PLEAT TAPE FOR TRIPLE PLEATS, OR FRENCH HEADING

This heading can be made by hand by using a fine buckram tape, or with the deep-pleat tape. This tape is applied like all the other tapes, but has special three-pronged hooks which you slide in the slots on the tape, to make the pleats. Two and a half times the length of the track is required for the fabric. This type of heading can cover your track, or lie under it, according to the type of hooks you get – one type has a short neck, the other a long neck, but both give the same heading effect.

A scalloped heading requires no tape and is useful for the kitchen. It can also be used as a door curtain to hang from a regency pole. You only need the exact length of the pole in fabric, but the hooks have to be sewn on. They are brass hooks, obtainable at most furnishing stores.

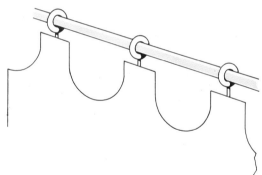

Measuring

LENGTH

Always put the track or curtain pole in position first, to enable you to get the exact measurements.

1. Measure from the base of the ring for the hook, on the track, to your required length. Short curtains look better 10–15cm/4–6in. beneath the sill, floor-length curtains should be within 13mm/½in. of the floor or carpet.

2. Measure from the base of the hook, on the track, to the required height (if there is no pelmet), to enable the track to be hidden when the curtains are drawn.

Add these two measurements together to find the overall length of the curtain, adding 20–23cm/8–9in. for the hem and the heading.

If the window is in a recess or alcove with the track set on the wall, and you want the curtains to rest above the sill, measure the length as for the long curtains, i.e. 13mm/½in. above the sill.

Therefore to find your required length, you need:

Hook drop + heading + hem and turnings

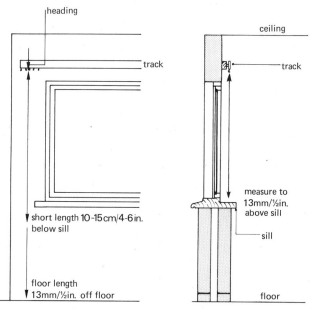

WIDTH

The amount of material needed for a pair of curtains depends on three things:

1. The type of heading chosen.
2. The type, or weight of material.
3. Rufflette tape requires 1½ times the length of curtain track or rod. Regis tape, deep-pleat tape, or french headings require 2–2½ times the length of rod.

Curtain fabrics generally come in 122–137cm/48–54in. widths, therefore, always calculate your widths in 122cm/48in. lengths. I have made an approximate chart for you to follow, showing the different amounts required according to fabric type. Light-weight fabrics are especially suitable for small windows, where space is limited. Heavy-weight materials are best suited to large windows, and where there is plenty of draw-back space.

If there is no draw-back space, drapes, made from half a width per curtain, and a shaped pelmet blind in the same or a contrasting fabric, can look most effective.

RUFFLETTE TAPE

Fabric	*Track length* 1.22m/4ft.	1.82m/6ft.	2.03m/8ft.	5.33m/10ft.
Number of *widths required*				
Net	2–3	3–4	4	5
Light-weight	2	3	3	4
Heavy	2	2–3	3	3–4

REGIS TAPE AND FRENCH HEADINGS

Fabric	*Track length* 1.22m/4ft.	1.82m/6ft.	2.03m/8ft.	5.33m/10ft.
Number of *widths required*				
Net	2–3	3–4	5	5–6
Light-weight	2	3–4	4–5	5
Heavy	2	3	4	5

Cutting and joining for 1½ widths per curtain

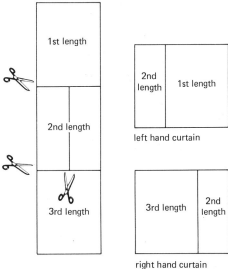

1st length

2nd length

3rd length

2nd length | 1st length

left hand curtain

3rd length | 2nd length

right hand curtain

PATTERNED FABRICS

Most designs on patterned fabrics, match equally on either side of the selvage, but some do not, and have what is called a 'pattern drop',

both half flowers match

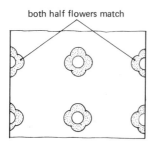

'pattern drop'

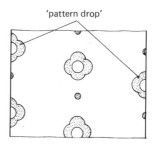

When purchasing a fabric with a 'pattern drop', do remember to allow enough for this drop. The diagram shown here illustrates the cutting and assembling for a pair of curtains, with $1\frac{1}{2}$ widths per curtain, showing where you need this extra material.

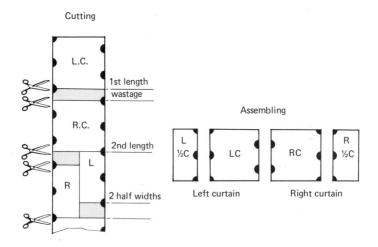

Machined unlined curtains

Hook drop 142cm/56in.   157cm/58in. over all length.
Heading 5cm/2in.
$1\frac{1}{2}$ widths per curtain.

1. Cut three lengths 168cm/66in. long (this allows 20cm/8in. for hem and heading turnings). Cut one in half lengthways.

2. Join the half widths to the whole widths by machine, joining the selvage edges only. Make sure the half width is on the outer side of each curtain.

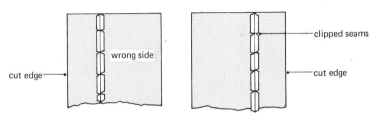

3. Clip seamed edges about 10cm/4in. apart. This will allow the seams to drop when the curtain is hung, and prevent it looking tight. Press seams open.

4. Turn the outer edges in 19mm/$\frac{3}{4}$in., and over again. Machine. Press.

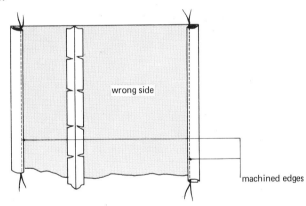

5. *Hem*

Turn up 15cm/6in. for hem, turning under 6cm/2$\frac{1}{2}$in.

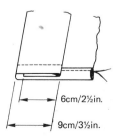

6. Machine across hem and down both open ends.

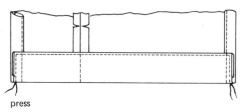

press

7. Lay out curtain on large, even, flat surface, and measure along curtain from hem to heading, the length 157cm/56in., just with pins at the top.

8. Turn over the top heading where pins are, and re-pin.

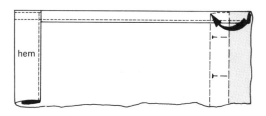

9. Place Rufflette tape on top of heading, and machine along top first, tucking under the raw edge about 2.5cm/1in. at both ends. Make sure that it measures 5cm/2in. from the *top* of the Rufflette pockets, to the top of the curtain. This will then give the 5cm/2in. heading to cover the track.

Machine along the base of the Rufflette, ensuring that you machine across the centre open end to hold the ties, but *NOT* the outer end, as these are the ties you will be using to draw up the heading.

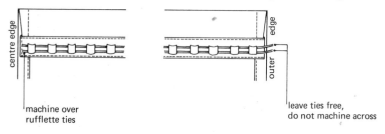

machine over
rufflette ties

leave ties free,
do not machine across

The curtains are now completed. All that is left to be done is to draw the end Rufflette ties up to equal the length of the track.

If the track is 213cm/84in. long, each curtain must be drawn up to 109cm/43in., the extra 2.5cm/1in. allows a little bit of give, so that they don't leave a gap in the centre when drawn.

Put your hooks in the Rufflette pockets, about 10–12.5cm/4–5in. apart, and hang.

This is a basic method for all machined curtains, whether they have Rufflette or any other type of heading.

FLAT SEAM

Some people prefer a flat centre seam.

1. Clip selvage 10–15.2cm/4–5in. apart.

2. Place right sides together, with the top width 6mm/¼in. from the bottom width.

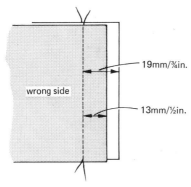

3. Machine 13mm/½in. in, on the top width.

4. Press open.

5. Then press again with the wider edge on top.

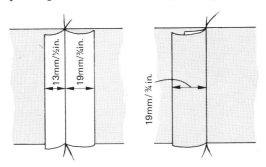

6. Turn under 6mm/¼in. on the wide edge and machine.

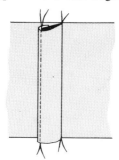

7. Press.

Lined curtains

Hook drop 142cm/56in.
Heading 5cm/2in.   } 157cm/58in. overall length.
1½ widths per curtain.

    1. Cut three lengths of material 168cm/66in. long.
Cut one length in half down centre.
    2. Cut three lengths of lining 157cm/62in. long.
Cut one length in half down centre.

LINING

    3. Machine both lining halves to whole widths. Press open seams.
    4. Turn up 7.5cm/3in. for hem, turn under 4cm/1½in. and machine straight across. Make sure that the half widths are on the outer sides of the curtain.

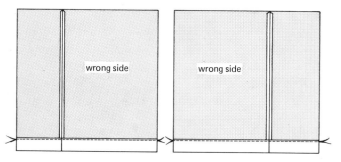

Press linings, and set aside.

MATERIAL

    5. Join both material halves to whole widths, clip selvages 10–12.5cm/4–5in. apart, and press seams open.
    6. Using the largest table possible, lay curtain right side down, and pin side seams in 4cm/1½in., and with large 5–7.5cm/2–3in. hem

stitches, baste, to within 23–25cm/9–10in. of the bottom of curtain. Pick up only one thread of the curtain so that it is invisible on the right side.

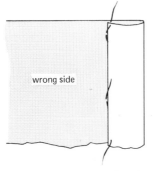

7. Turn up hem 15cm/6in., turning under 7cm/2¾in., giving you a 8cm/3¼in. hem-line. Pin.

8. Mitre the corners, and pin. See diagram on page 82.

Full length lined curtain to hang under the pole. Thick cord and tassel have been used for a tie-back.

9. Stitch the mitred corner together with invisible stitches.
10. Stitch the hem, and mitre the other corner similarly.

A mitred corner

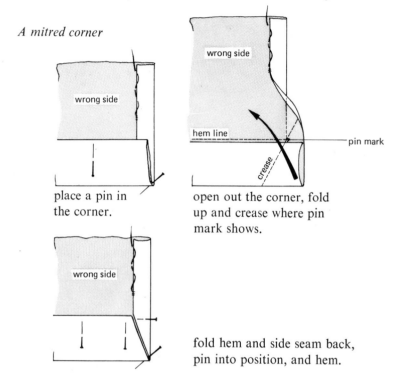

place a pin in
the corner.

open out the corner, fold
up and crease where pin
mark shows.

fold hem and side seam back,
pin into position, and hem.

JOINING LINING TO CURTAIN

1. Place the curtain material face down on the table, and put the
correct lining, wrong side down, on top of it 19–25mm/$\frac{3}{4}$–1in. above
the curtain material hem line.

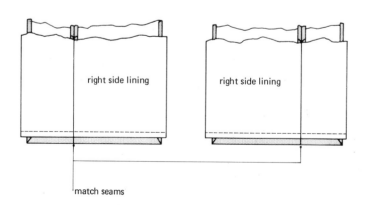

2. Turn the half width back, and lock the selvages together with a large loose buttonhole stitch, to the hem. Attach the top of both hems with a loose buttonhole chain stitch.

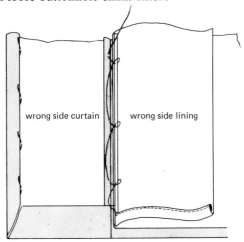

wrong side curtain   wrong side lining

3. Turn the other half width over and repeat. Fold the two halves back again, turn the edges in about 19–25mm/¾in–1in. from the curtain edges and hem.

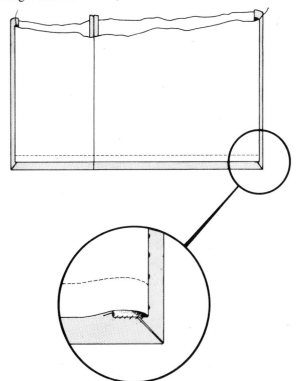

HEADING

Measure curtain 157cm/58in. from hem to top, at about 10cm/4in. intervals, and turn down both raw edges together.

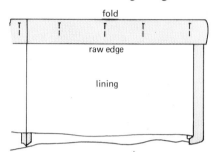

Machine tape on, turning under 25cm/1in. at both ends. Leave tape strings free at the outer edge (half width side) for drawing the curtain up afterwards. Make sure that it measures 5cm/2in. from the top of the tape hook pockets, to the top of the curtain. This is the heading which has previously been measured, to allow the curtain to cover the track.

Draw up the tape strings so that both curtains measure the length of the track, e.g. if track is 213cm/84in. draw each curtain up to 109cm/43in.

Place your hooks 10–12.5cm/4–5in. apart and hang.

Almost all lined curtains are made this way, varying only in widths and lengths. Depending on which heading you choose all the tapes are applied with the same method, except for the hand-sewn french headings.

Velour curtains need special treatment. Because of the thickness of material, turn the hem up once only and herring-bone stitch the hem.

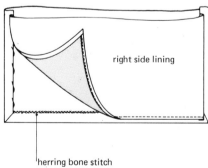

8. Tie-backs

These are useful for many reasons, mainly to allow more light into the room. Long curtains beside a french window, or door, can be prevented from being blown about, as well as looking more decorative.

They can be simply made from an oddment of braid or tasselling, gilt chains, or a strip of the same material tied around and attached to the wall over a hook. Decorative chains, tie-back and round holdbacks, can be bought at most furnishing stores, obtainable in a selection of colours, brass, pewter, antique brass and white.

Soft tie-backs, self-lined, or with a contrasting lining, tied around once, need no wall attachments, and look most effective, especially on frilled bedroom net curtains.

Shaped tie-back

Measure the length required with a piece of string or tape. Draw the shape required on a stiffener, preferably buckram, and cut out.

If the material you are using is light-weight or sheer, cover the shaped buckram with a light-weight interlining, and stitch or stick the overlapping edges to the back, using a fabric adhesive like Copydex.

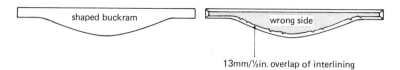

shaped buckram

wrong side

13mm/½in. overlap of interlining

Cut your covering material 13mm/½in. larger than the shape, place it over the interlining, and stitch or stick in place on the back.

Cut a piece of lining 13mm/½in. larger than the shape. Press a 19mm/¾in. seam all round, clipping any curves.

Pin the lining onto the back, and handsew with a small hemstitch, onto the stuck or stitched overlapped edges.

lining

Join the ends, lining on the inside, oversewing them together. A split ring (obtainable at Woolworths, and most large furnishing stores, in various sizes), can then be slipped around the end, for attaching to a brass hook on the wall.

Ensure both the hooks are at the same level.

This type of tie-back is ideal for curtains that are not drawn, but are for decoration. If they are in constant use, do not join the ends together, but sew them individually around two brass rings. This will enable you to release one side of the tie-back, leaving it hanging behind the curtain, when they are drawn.

Joined with a split ring

Joined with two rings

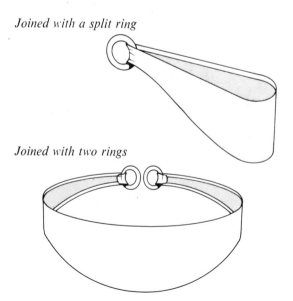